-est as in nest

Nancy Tuminelly

Consulting Editor Monica Marx, M.A./Reading Specialist

Published by SandCastle™, an imprint of ABDO Publishing Company, 4940 Viking Drive, Edina, Minnesota 55435.

Printed in the United States.

Credits
Edited by: Pam Price
Curriculum Coordinator: Nancy Tuminelly
Cover and Interior Design and Production: Mighty Media
Photo Credits: Brand X Pictures, Comstock, Corbis Images, Eyewire Images, Hemera, Image Ideas Inc., PhotoDisc, Rubberball Productions, Stockbyte

Library of Congress Cataloging-in-Publication Data

Tuminelly, Nancy, 1952-
    -Est as in nest / Nancy Tuminelly.
      p. cm. -- (Word families. Set II)
    Summary: Introduces, in brief text and illustrations, the use of the letter combination "est" in such words as "nest," "chest," "test," and "guest."
    ISBN 1-59197-232-9
    1. Readers (Primary) [1. Vocabulary. 2. Reading.] I. Title. II. Series.

PE1119 .T824 2003
428.1--dc21   2002038621

SandCastle™ books are created by a professional team of educators, reading specialists, and content developers around five essential components that include phonemic awareness, phonics, vocabulary, text comprehension, and fluency. All books are written, reviewed, and leveled for guided reading, early intervention reading, and Accelerated Reader® programs and designed for use in shared, guided, and independent reading and writing activities to support a balanced approach to literacy instruction.

Let Us Know

After reading the book, SandCastle would like you to tell us your stories about reading. What is your favorite page? Was there something hard that you needed help with? Share the ups and downs of learning to read. We want to hear from you! To get posted on the ABDO Publishing Company Web site, send us e-mail at:

sandcastle@abdopub.com

SandCastle Level: Beginning

-est Words

chest

crest

nest

pest

test

vest

There are lots of toys in the chest.

The top of a wave is
called a crest.

Josh gently holds the nest.

Erin is being a pest to her dad.

Amy is taking a test.

Mike is wearing a life vest.

The Guest from the West

We have
a guest.

He came
from the West.

The name of
our guest
is Mr. Fest.

Mr. Fest brought
his things in
an old chest.

Mom showed
Mr. Fest
where to take
off his vest.

Then Mr. Fest lay
down for a rest.

I didn't want
to be a pest.

So I went
to my room
to study for
a test.

When our guest,
Mr. Fest,
got up from
his rest,
he gave us
a bird's nest.

We were happy
to have Mr. Fest
as our guest.

He was the best!

We said goodbye to Mr. Fest.

It was time for him to head back out West.

The -est Word Family

best	quest
chest	rest
crest	test
guest	vest
jest	west
nest	zest
pest	

Glossary

Some of the words in this list may have more than one meaning. The meaning listed here reflects the way the word is used in the book.

chest   a large, sturdy box, often with a lid and a lock, used for storage

crest   the top of a hill or a wave; the upright feathers on top of a bird's head

guest   a person who has been invited to another's home

nest   a shelter made by birds or other animals to keep their eggs and babies safe

About SandCastle™

A professional team of educators, reading specialists, and content developers created the SandCastle™ series to support young readers as they develop reading skills and strategies and increase their general knowledge. The SandCastle™ series has four levels that correspond to early literacy development in young children. The levels are provided to help teachers and parents select the appropriate books for young readers.

Emerging Readers
(no flags)

Beginning Readers
(1 flag)

Transitional Readers
(2 flags)

Fluent Readers
(3 flags)

These levels are meant only as a guide. All levels are subject to change.

ABDO Publishing Company

To see a complete list of SandCastle™ books and other nonfiction titles from ABDO Publishing Company, visit **www.abdopub.com** or contact us at:

4940 Viking Drive, Edina, Minnesota 55435 • 1-800-800-1312 • fax: 1-952-831-1632